Lord,

What Are You Doing

Next Tuesday?

Feb 19, 1986
Ruby & Ernie

Hope you enjoy the
antics of "Sarah
Elizabeth" (see
Preface) We
laughed alot!
Love you —
Merle & Jim

Lord, What Are You Doing Next Tuesday?

by Ona Brigham Dukes

The Bethany Press
St. Louis, Missouri

Illustrated by Beverly Johnston

Library of Congress Cataloging in Publication Data
Dukes, Ona Brigham.
  Lord, what are you doing next Tuesday?

  1. Meditations. I. Title.
BV4832.2.D77   242   78-17343
ISBN: 0-8272-2114-2
ISBN-0-8272-2115-0 pbk. (Special Edition)

Distributed in Canada by The G.R. Welch Company, Ltd., Toronto, Ontario, Canada.

Printed in the United States of America

Dedicated to my
father and mother,
Walter and Lena Firth

Preface

Hi. I'm Sarah Elizabeth. My Daddy is a preacher. He doesn't do anything except on Sundays. Sundays is when we all stand and say Our Father, who art in Heaven, Hello! What be Thy name?

I hope you will read my book. It's all about me and the Lord Almighty talking. But if you expect to find out who is the Lord Almighty's mother, or what God stood on when he created the world —don't read it. It isn't in here.

But if you want to know about the Lord Almighty and me, and about all the kissing at weddings, and about Moses roasting the hot dogs, then go ahead. It's OK.

Love,

Sarah Elizabeth

Contents

Chapter 1

Beginnings

Lord, some day I would like to talk to you about how you made everything. I would like to know what the ant was before he was an ant. And when you built those big mountains, did you start with one little old rock and go up from there? Did you carry them all by yourself, or did someone let you have his wheelbarrow? Also I would like to know why you didn't make better weather, especially on Christmas and birthdays.

Excuse me, but in Genesis you shouldn't have divided the light. Then you could have seen what you were doing better. That's probably why the elephant's feet are so big. If I had been there, I would have loaned you my father's flashlight. Next time you'd better use one—at least for the big things.

If you wouldn't make quite so many animals, it sure would help. Then we wouldn't have so many in school. I missed "guraffe" three times on a spelling test. Just keep it simple with some horses and pigs and a duck and a chicken. You notice I left out the mosquito, which is a good thing. Mrs. Cronk says the way they sting,

they must be the work of the devil. That makes me feel better. I sure would feel bad if I knew you did it. Did the devil make the skunk, too? He isn't really nice either, you know.

Mr. Hoffhiser at the store says some people are too mean to be born. How do you take care of things like that? I thought everybody was born and that's that. Like Lydia June Stillwater. She knows where she was born. It was at Mercy Hospital. Her mother was visiting someone at the time and just picked her up. Johnny Belcher said he was born in the back seat of the car while everybody was out riding around and eating ice cream cones. I know where I was. I was home all alone at the time. My father was out calling, and my mother was at a missionary meeting.

I would like to ask you to do something. Lydia June's mother is going to go on an airplane next week. She said she sure would feel better if the Almighty was by her side. I was wondering what you are doing next Tuesday. Could you maybe be with her? If you let everybody know ahead, you might even get to fly the plane. That would make her feel good.

And the next time you are making things, could you please make some nice covers for kids' elbows? It's awful hard leaning on them to watch the ants crawl through the crack in the sidewalk. Thank you very much.

P.S. The next time you are hanging around creating, could we kids watch? We always get sent from the room just as good things happen—like opening the potato chips or putting up the Christmas tree.

Chapter 2

Weddings

A wedding is where a man and lady stand up in front of everybody including the Father, Son and Holy Ghost. Then my father says, "Do you?" and they both say, "We do." Then the man puts a ring on her hand and says, "I love you, even if you are better or worse." She gets to tell him the same thing back. They go down on their knees while Agnes Struble sings "I Love You Truly in the Key of C." Then he kisses her, and everybody cries until they go to Niagara Falls.

Some weddings have only four people in them. Others have lots—even twelve sometimes. I think that is so they remember they are really married. I like these weddings the best. It means there is always more jello downstairs afterwards, especially strawberry.

After a wedding, my mother is always happy. I think it is because she gets the money that my father gets for all the bother. One time a man came to the door with two dead rabbits. It was to pay for his bride, he said. Mother laughed and said just be glad it isn't skunks. I hope my husband doesn't pay for me in rabbits. I think I'll try to

15

get him to make it two camels from darkest Africa. That might help the missionaries.

Some ladies are very silly when they get married. Some giggle and others chew gum. One of them fainted dead away, and Mrs. Gillespie had to play "Revive Us Again" till they could prop her up.

At real special weddings, Father also gives them the bread and grape juice. I don't mind this except at hot weddings. Then everyone gets thirsty just watching. Most of the time, though, they are just short ones. The man and lady are always anxious to get to Niagara Falls so everybody can quit crying.

Sometimes we have "stand-up" weddings in our house. This is where they knock on our door, walk in and stand up to get married. If they sat down, I don't think the Father and the Son would mind, but maybe the Holy Ghost wouldn't like it. He would have to hide in the fireplace because the room would be so crowded.

I think I like the "stand-ups" the best because I get to see them kiss up closer. That is, if my mother doesn't call me out to the kitchen first.

Last week I married Johnny Belcher to Lydia June Stillwater. We borrowed Mr. Hoffhiser's chicken coop behind his smokehouse. They held hands and I said, "Do you?" and they did. Then Johnny spoiled it because he wouldn't kiss her. He said Lydia June smelled like peanut butter, which always makes him throw up.

Lord, if you have weddings in Heaven, would you mind taking out all the crying and adding more of the kissing part? If you do, I would like to have a front-row seat. Also I would thank you if you would have lots of strawberry jello with bananas in it for us afterwards. This is cheaper than grape juice, especially at the hot weddings.

Chapter 3

Gossip

Mrs. Cronk, my Sunday school teacher, says that gossip is what you hear and believe—that someone doesn't say. I've sat around all day trying to hear things people didn't say, but I haven't heard anything.

Mrs. Cronk says gossip is what gets you in trouble even when you haven't done anything. That's because gossip comes in two kinds, she says—third and fourth hand. I guess kids can't gossip because they have only two hands. I just wonder where grown-ups keep their third and fourth hands, because they sure don't show anywhere. Old Mr. Appleby, who sits in front of us every Sunday morning, has a hump in the middle of his back. I have wondered if this was a third or fourth hand. I would tap him if my mother wasn't looking.

Grown-ups also have another thing they say. They say, "Don't let your left hand know what your right hand is doing." Last week my left hand held a cooky, and my right hand knew it all the time. Next time I will hide my cooky behind my back.

Mother says gossip is passed on by people who are too busy to work for the Lord but are not too busy to talk about the sinners, which includes everybody. Because when they get through talking, even the "sent" and the "chosen" are sinners also.

One Sunday Father put in big letters at the top of the church bulletin: "What every church needs is bigger and better mouth traps." The next day I asked Mr. Hoffhiser down at the store if I could maybe buy a mouth trap. He said—was that anything like a bear trap—one step and you're a goner. I said no because that worked on the wrong end, I think. He scratched his bald head, and said he would be sure to save me a mouth trap if an order of them came in.

I will not put anything more down on this subject. My father says when it comes to gossip, the less said the better. I will not say anything more because I would like to be on the side of the better. I hope that is right next to the "chosen."

P.S. Lord, maybe if I had said less, it would have been better.

Chapter 4

Saints and Sinners

Saints are people who wash their robes in the blood—I think. I guess that could mean living people, too. Mother leans over on Sunday morning and whispers to Mrs. Cronk, "Look at Mr. Simpkin sitting over there. Isn't he a dear old saint?"

I look at old Mr. Simpkin. His bald head shines all green from the church window. The egg stains on his shirt look green too. Even when I squeeze my eyes half shut, I can't see him in a long white robe washed in the blood. Maybe I will be mighty surprised when I get to Heaven and see him sitting between Moses and Abraham.

Also, it will have to be up to somebody else to play his harp because old Mr. Simpkin can't read a note. He just sits and holds his songbook and watches Miss Juliah in the choir.

I don't think I know about the saints. But there are three other kinds I do know about. These are the sinners and the "sent" and the "chosen." The sinners are easy ones because everybody points them out. The "sent" are the ones the Lord Almighty picks out before they arrive. And the "chosen" are the ones who have to be told where to go after they get here.

The "sent" are the people who sit around and tell other people how to do things. Like Burt Peasley. He says he sure would like to tell people where to go sometimes. That means that Burt Peasley is one of the "sent," I think. Father says Burt Peasley had better enjoy putting coal in his furnace here because he sure is going to do a lot of it later. I've looked in the Bible, and I don't find anything about furnaces. Maybe it is where the seraphim get the hot coals to carry around. If I am a seraphim, I will say thank you when Burt Peasley hands me a hot coal.

I wish I knew if I am a "sent" or a "chosen." I would ask Mrs. Cronk, my Sunday school teacher, but she doesn't know either. I heard her tell Miss Gittle, who hands out our crayons, "I just don't know about that child." Since then, I have tried to help her know me better. Like lending her my best white handkerchief or licking her stamps before she needs them.

Till I grow up, I will have to carry a mirror around with me. That is so that I can keep checking. I have done this since I heard Mrs. Stillwater talking to my mother. She said most preachers' kids turn out to be the "black sheep" of the family. I sure hope I hurry and grow up fast. How could I explain this to the other kids in the block?

Lord, If I did turn into a black sheep, could this keep me from sitting on my right hand? Even if I keep practicing during the sermon so it doesn't bother me anymore?

Chapter 5

Parsonages

A parsonage is a place where the minister lives. It is a place that the "sent" and the "chosen" give things to—like a horsehair sofa in the study and the wicker rocker with the squeaky bottom. I think people give these things to keep from sinning. They say, "It would be a sin to throw it away," so they give it to the minister.

Sometimes the sinners give things too. Father said it would take an old sinner like Burt Peasley to give something like the hand-carved statue of St. Peter. He holds our hats in the front hall. Father said that's probably the closest Burt Peasley will ever get to St. Peter. I don't understand this because I thought St. Peter meets everybody at the gate. Maybe Mr. Peasley knows of another way to get in.

A parsonage is also a place where everybody wants to be. Like the Ladies' Aid, the Official Board and the Missionary Society. They come in and they say, "Isn't it lovely we have given our minister such a nice home to meet in?"

A parsonage is a place where all the choir kids pull taffy on Thursday nights and where everyone tiptoes on Saturday because Father

is getting the Word from the Lord for Sunday. It is also where the church Halloween parties are held because the Lord doesn't appreciate the raw liver and the peeled grapes that are passed. Neither does anybody else, so they all come to the parsonage.

A parsonage keeps other people's things, too. Like the church keys, the choir music and the Communion grape juice. I would like to tell you something about me and the grape juice one time. But that is just between me and the Lord—I think.

I like to live in a parsonage because we get to keep all the people that come. Like the Bishop and the missionary from China. One time we even got to keep Mr. Lwamba from Africa. He came to tell us that people must love everybody like God said, but Mother said that sermon ended at the church door. That is why we got to keep him at the parsonage. I don't know what door sermons are supposed to end at. I have looked them all over, but it beats me. That is another question I must ask the Lord when I see him.

A parsonage is a place where even before the moving van backs up, Mother says, "Walter, go down and buy some oatmeal wallpaper. The rooms sure need it." Mother says that oatmeal wallpaper goes with anything. Like the horsehair sofa, the flowered rug and the next minister's wife. I hope they run out of oatmeal wallpaper before I grow up and get married. Then I can have some with big cabbage roses and bluebirds on it.

Lord, I would like to thank you for keeping quiet about the Communion grape juice. I want you to know I will do the same.

Chapter 6

The Hereafter

The "hereafter" is where you go to get a rest from the "henceforth." I know this because my father is always going from the "henceforth" to the "hereafter" in his sermons. It is also the place where you wear a long white robe washed in the blood, and you sit on the right hand. During long sermons, I sit on my right hand to get ready for the "hereafter," but it isn't very comfortable. I hope it will be more so in Heaven.

I don't mind the robes and the harps, even though I can't play one, but I don't think I can sleep there. I know this because we sing a song about "there shall be no night there." My room must be real dark for me to sleep. Maybe the cherubim and the seraphim will help me with this.

I wish I knew how to become a cherubim. I think I would like that better than a seraphim because they just fly around all the time with hot coals in their hands. They even did this the day that the train the Lord was riding filled the temple. I know because it says, "I

saw the Lord high and lifted up and his train filled the temple.''
What for, I do not know. But it says so in the Bible.

I know Heaven must be full of wonderful surprises. But I do not
know if they are the Christmas kind or the birthday kind. All I know
is that my Sunday school teacher says some people will be mighty
surprised when they get there.

I can hardly wait to see the pearly gates and the golden streets
and pick out my mansion. I hope it isn't a place like the parsonage
where Mother always says, ''Hurry now and pick everything up.
You never know who might come to the door.'' I also hope no one
has to give me a horsehair sofa to keep from sinning. I really don't
think I want one up there.

My father says everybody is happy in Heaven because they can
do what they want. I wonder if the Lord Almighty will play Chinese
Checkers or Old Maid with me? If the Lord has too many things to
do, maybe Abraham will. If he does, I'll bet I can beat him.

P.S. Lord, I will gladly give up my seraphim seat for a cherubim one
if someone would like to swap with me, that is. Even if it means sitting on my right hand, it will be worth it.

Chapter 7

Sunday School

Sunday school is where everybody says good morning to each other. Then the teacher gives you a piece of paper and a crayon. And she tells you to think and then draw a line around it. It is also where you make things for the poor heathen and you listen to Bible stories.

Today in Sunday school the lesson was about Jonah and the whale. You know, the man who didn't go where the Lord Almighty told him to go. Maybe he didn't know he was supposed to be one of the "sent."

Anyway, there was a big storm, and Jonah got thrown over and a big whale came swishing along and swallowed him up. In a few days the Lord Almighty came along and talked to the whale. And the whale was just sick about it.

That's as far as we got because it was time to make rolls for the missionary box. We each take skinny pieces of white rag and roll them up. I do not know what the heathen do with these. Maybe it has something to do with the song "When the Roll Is Called up

Yonder, I'll Be There." I sure hope I am there when it is called. I want to see what they do with them.

Sunday school teachers spend half the time telling us how to do unto others, and the other half practicing us for Rally Day. Rally Day is when the kindergarten kids get up and sing so their mothers can come up and get them because they won't come down.

Rally Day is when you say everything you know and you sing everything you have heard. Like "the blesseds" and the "thou shalt nots" and "Jesus Wants Me for a Sunbeam."

Last year Lydia June Stillwater got to sing "Yes, Jesus Loves Me." Her father is one of the "sent," I think. Lydia June was waving at her mother so hard, she forgot the last line. She sang:

"Yes, Jesus loves me,
Yes, Jesus loves me,
Yes, Jesus loves me,
Only the Lord knows why."

I think I like her verse the best.

If they would let children teach Sunday school, everybody would learn a lot more things. Besides, they wouldn't get people all mixed up. Like when Mrs. Cronk kept Janie McIntyre while her mother went shopping. It was the day old Mr. Simons was riding by in his casket. I don't know what Mrs. Cronk told Janie about what was going on. All I know is Janie wouldn't say her prayers that night. She said the Lord would be too busy unpacking that man they sent upstairs to listen to her.

Lord, someday I will be a Sunday school teacher maybe. Then I will tell everybody about Jonah and the whale and make chocolate-covered raisins for the heathen. I think they would like that better.

Chapter 8

Moses

Janie Stillwater told us about Moses the other day in Sunda school. I like the way the Lord took care of Moses. He gave him a pil lar of fire to see with. I guess maybe that's because the electric lights didn't work.

And Moses got to talk to the Lord Almighty any old time he felt like it. He would just climb the mountain, pull up a stool and say, "Well, Lord, what shall we talk about today?"

One day the Lord said, "Moses, I got a couple or ten things I think you need to know about." And he started right in.

Moses said, "Wait a minute, Lord, I can't remember all that. You'd better write them down."

Well, the Lord Almighty looked and saw a couple of writing tablets and a ballpoint pen hanging around under some bushes. He said, "I guess it will do." So he took up the ballpoint pen and just started writing. And Moses just sat there and sat there with his chin in his hands. By the time the Lord Almighty got through writing, he had two whole tablets full.

Moses said, "That's kind of long, Lord. You sure just one tablet won't do?"

The Lord Almighty said, "It's gotta be the whole thing. How'd you like a story that's only half finished?"

And Moses sighed and said OK. And he carried the two tablets down the mountainside.

What he didn't know was the people had gotten kind of tired hanging around. They had played dominoes and Kick the Can and Monopoly. And then someone said, "Let's build something." They looked around, but there wasn't anything—no Tinker Toys or even erector sets or Lincoln Logs. There was nothing but plain old dirt and trees.

So one of them said, "Go around and get some false teeth and all the old stuff people have. And we'll build a big fire and do some melting." So the people did. And they made a golden calf.

When Moses came down and saw it, he said, "Now, what did you go and do that for?"

If they had made it out of candy, at least all the kids could have broken off a piece to eat now and then. That's probably what Moses was thinking, too, because he had been a little boy himself once.

Lydia June said that at least the calf wasn't made of spinach. Janie said shut up. She wasn't finished with the story yet.

Well, Moses was mad and he kept getting madder and madder. He got so mad, he just stood up and threw the tablets on the ground. I don't see how they broke, though. Lydia June and I took our school tablets the next day and we threw them and threw them on the ground. But they just came out all in a mess. Maybe Moses had a different kind of ground.

Well, anyway, Moses cut the calf up into little pieces and put it in the water. Then he made the people drink it. Right then, Johnnie Belcher said "Yuck!" Janie Stillwater said it couldn't be as bad as her cod liver oil.

Anyway, it all came out all right. Janie said everybody got to roast hot dogs over the leftover fire.

Mrs. Cronk said it wasn't exactly the way Janie told it. She looks awful old—even forty maybe. She couldn't have been with Moses though because she still has her false teeth. I can hear them clicking when she sings "Jesus Wants Me for a Sunbeam."

P.S. Lord, I think you ought to know that a writing tablet doesn't break when you throw it on the ground. You ought to know that before you write any more stories. I would be glad to help you if you just let me know. You probably don't know these things because maybe you were never seven years old.

34

Chapter 9

Baptisms

In my church a baptism is when you get carried up to the altar in a long white dress. My father talks to the Lord Almighty and then you get carried over to a bowl of water down in a hole in a table. In some other churches, I hear, they dunk you in a pool. You have to be sure the Father, Son and Holy Ghost are there because they have a part in it.

One Saturday, I was in the church, pew-sliding with Lydia June. Mr. Berriman, the janitor, came along and said maybe the Lord Almighty wouldn't like that. To make up for it, he said I could carry the bowl for sprinkling down to the church kitchen and fill it. I will have to have a long talk with the Lord Almighty, because it sure did upset me. All the time, I thought that water came from the River Jordan.

Lydia June wouldn't play with her Christmas doll until we baptized it. We sure didn't want her starting out to be a sinner.

We sneaked over on Saturday before my father sprinkled on Sunday. I had gone through all of the "gathered togethers" and had

Lydia June's doll over the sprinkling bowl. Then we heard Mr. Berriman coming in the back door. Lydia June jerked me away so hard that her doll's eyes fell out and dropped in the sprinkling water. We waited and waited to get back in again, but the janitor never did come out.

In church the next morning, I tried not to notice when my father looked down in the water. I hope he thought it was the Holy Ghost's eyes looking up at him. I'm sure it wouldn't have happened with River Jordan water like it says in the Bible.

Mrs. Cronk says people who don't get sprinkled don't get to Heaven. If that is true, Noah sure must have made it. And Jonah, too. But I sure do worry about Isaiah. He just sat around with ashes on him all the time. Maybe that was dried up water, so it was OK.

I'm sure glad I was sprinkled. Now, all I have to worry about is the hardened sinner part. I shall keep pinching to make sure.

Lord, when you write some more new stories, will you explain about the River Jordan part? It sure would make all of us kids feel better. I don't want to hurt your feelings any, but we sure could use some new stories. When do you think you could get around to it? We sure are getting tired of the old ones.

Chapter 10

The Lord's Pictures

We have stopped making rolls for the heathen now. Mrs. Cronk wants us to work on pictures for the art show. She says if we do well, the Lord will be real pleased. Maybe he will give us an "A" like he did Moses for coming up after the tablets.

My father says the church has to keep finding new ways all the time. I am not sure for what. We have to just keep finding them. I asked Mrs. Cronk if there was a new way for Burt Peasley to stop his drinking habit. She said if there was, she'd sure be glad to hear it.

I like Dillon's picture the best. He drew Mary and Joseph fleeing into Egypt. He has a big, red airplane with four people in it. There's Mary and Joseph and the dear little Lord Jesus. And Pontius, the pilot.

Lydia June drew a big car with a man in the front seat and two people in back. Mrs. Cronk said, "Who is it, Lydia June?"

She said, "It's the Lord driving Adam and Eve out of the garden."

I said, "Oh, dear me, Lydia June." And quick, I drew in the Holy Ghost in the front seat. It would never do to hurt his feelings.

Matthew drew the biggest ark I ever saw. It was so big, it drew itself right off the paper. He put a nice big TV aerial on top of it. Noah must have gotten awful tired waiting for all that water to go somewhere.

Celia couldn't draw a whale, she said. Every time it came out looking like a balloon. So she just drew Jonah after the whale threw him up. He is wiping himself off before starting out for Cinema. Mrs. Cronk says that's the most important part anyway.

I wonder what Jonah ate when he was in the whale? Maybe the whale swallowed some bologna sandwiches to help Jonah out.

I drew Ezekiel and his wheel. I thought it was pretty good until Johnny Belcher said it looked like a hula hoop. The Lord Almighty won't laugh because he knows what I'm thinking.

P.S. Lord, I hope you let the whale into Heaven. How did he know Jonah had someplace special to go?

38

Chapter 11

Revival Meetings

Every year—like after Christmas or just before spring—my father gets the "revivaling spirit." My mother gets all upset and red in the face. She says "religion isn't something one wears on one's sleeve." I have looked over all the sleeves in my closet. And I must be all right because there is nothing on them.

Revival meetings are where everyone gets all excited and shouts and cries. And no matter what the weather is outside, it always gets hot inside. This is where "Just As I Am" is sung until your throat gets sore. "One more chorus," Father says, and the organist sighs and starts in again.

One time my father was going through it "one more time" and Mrs. Bixby was just passing me by in the aisle. Her hands were up and she was saying, "I'm coming, Lord, I'm coming." Right about then the lights went out. Maybe it was the Holy Spirit or something.

Father said, "Now, everyone coming forward to be saved, stay right where you are till you are sure where you are going." The lights never did come on again, even with the Lord and the janitor's help.

And everyone had to wait until the next night so they could be sure where they were going.

Father said you could always tell the saints from the sinners at revival meetings because the saints would always come forward and the sinners would stay glued to their seats. Father would thump on the pulpit and shout, "There is nothing more displeasing to the Lord than a hardened sinner. The Holy Spirit is waiting for you right down at this altar rail."

I would pinch my arms, and I could find nothing hard about them except around the wrist part. So I knew I was safe in my pew, and the Holy Spirit wasn't waiting for me.

Mother said that after revivals, people had awful short memories. She said she was talking about "the regulars" that always came forward. The only thing regular about them, she said, was the way they could forget their revivaling and just go back to the way they were before. Like Mr. Wilson, who had seven children and a talking parrot. He is the kind Father said "got the wrong kind of spirit." All I know is he would come in afterwards and borrow money from Father so he could settle his account with the Lord. Mother's nose would wrinkle up all funny. Then she would say the day that man settled his account, something would freeze over. I never did find out what that was. I think that is one of the questions I shall have to ask the Lord when I see him after I cross over into Beulahland.

I hope I never get to be a hardened sinner. I'll just have to keep pinching to make sure. If I did become one, I would want to be the first to find out.

Chapter 12

Christmas

I like Christmas best of all. I just wish, though, it came twice a year so we wouldn't have to be good so long.

Last year I got to play Mary in the Christmas play. I had to sit by the manger and look down into the face of the dear little Lord Jesus. It was a little hard to pretend because they used Lydia June's old doll. It had cracks all over its face. Besides, it didn't swaddle very good in the clothes it had on. I knew the dear little Lord Jesus didn't look like that, but I pretended anyway.

I was glad when it was all over because I got a cramp in my leg. Maybe Mary got one, too. She sure must have sat a long time while all the shepherds and wise men and kings marched on by.

Last year, everybody got real upset with Dillon Long. He asked the teacher and asked the teacher if he could play the innkeeper. The teacher sighed and said she guessed so. At practice, Dillon had to shut the door in Mary's and Joseph's face. He always ended up crying 'cause he felt so bad. Mrs. Kittle said he had to try harder. Dillon kept trying till he sounded like a real sinner.

The night of the play when Mary and Joseph came knocking, he shouted at them to go away. Then he just looked at them standing there and said, "Oh, why don't you come in for a minute and have a beer?"

Mrs. Kittle jerked him off the stage, and Mrs. Cronk started playing "Here Comes the Bride" by mistake. I don't know why they did that. Dillon was only trying to help, and Mary and Joseph must have been thirsty after all that walking. Maybe Mrs. Cronk was upset because she didn't get to think of it.

I feel sorry for the innkeeper. How did he know what stars to look at? Besides, how could he keep track when he was so busy making ham sandwiches for everybody who came that night?

This year maybe the manger scene will be outdoors. If they can find a place, that is. Mr. Click said they could use his lot at the hardware store. Only thing is, they will have to cut down on the wise men and shepherds. He says it wouldn't look good to have them caught between the tractors and the wheelbarrows. My father's face got red. He said if they had to do that, it would be the last straw. That would really be too bad. What else would the dear little Lord Jesus lie on?

I wonder why the little Lord Jesus was born at such a busy time of the year? Even the "sent" and the "chosen" have trouble squeezing it in. Perhaps some day, the Lord Almighty will change Jesus' birthday to Halloween or the Fourth of July. Everyone could enjoy it better.

Lord, if no one can ever make a mistake like the innkeeper did, how can anyone get to Heaven except Moses and George Washington? I sure would like to know before I get there. Maybe you could send us a message through a miracle. My father says if he ever got a church without any hardened sinners, it would be a miracle. I know it would take some doing, but could you please arrange it? Maybe you could get Abraham to help you. He must be awful tired of playing his harp by now.

Chapter 13

And a Lot of Things

Johnny found a nest of pink mice yesterday. We all went over to see them. There they were—all pink and squealy. Johnny wondered how come they didn't have their coats on yet.

I said that's because you let them decide what color they will be. I thought you did a nice job on them. The pussy willows are pretty too. And the big green frog in Mr. Berriman's garden.

Lydia June says it must be awful crowded in Heaven by now. She and I have a good idea. Instead of making new people all the time, why don't you just keep the ones you got? Then everyone will get to have a lot more fun. And that way, we can stay kids longer. Besides, you wouldn't have to keep all the new ones stacked up somewhere. I sure would like to know where they come from, but no one will tell us.

Lydia June and I wonder what kids do while they are waiting to come here. If the streets of Heaven are all made of gold, where do they go to play hopscotch? I hope it's somewhere besides Jordan's stormy banks. All the chalk marks would get washed out.

Mrs. Cronk says if Burt Peasley ever gets into Heaven, he will sure have to pay a price. Is that something you left out telling us? I didn't know St. Peter collects at the door, but I'll sure start saving in my mite box.

Isn't it time you had some new miracles? The one I like the best is about making the camel walk through the eye of the needle. I sure wish I had been there. Couldn't you make our elbows so they would bend backwards? Or maybe make Johnny Belcher's sister pretty? It sure would help a lot. She's as mean and ugly as a skunk.

And another thing. Could you also show us what Heaven is like? Don't worry. I don't want to go there. I just want to know in case anybody asks.

P.S. I am doing the best I can. I hope you are doing the same.
P.P.S. I want you to know I am on your side.

Chapter 14

Noah and His Dear Little Ark

Mrs. Cronk read to us about Noah last week. The first part is real scary. It tells about the giants hanging around who had bare children. That is too bad, but I suppose Betsy Ross couldn't be everywhere. She had enough trouble sewing the flag.

It was nice when Noah found Grace in the eyes of the Lord. Grace must have been a real good wife to him, baking his bread and everything. Before Noah got on his dear little ark, I wonder where she did her shopping for all that kind? It says, "Every beast was after his kind." I asked Mr. Hofhiser at the grocery store if kind came in cans like dog food. He said, darned if he knew. But if I came across any, he'd offer it on a two-for-one-sale.

It sure must have been crowded sleeping in the ark. Maybe they had bunk beds with the elephants on the bottom and the fleas on the top.

Since Noah was 600 years old, maybe he was too tired to watch television. Grace probably said, "Go to bed, Noah. I have lots of company."

Then the Lord noticed one day that the windows of Heaven were all stopped up. So he unplugged one and leaned out and yelled, "Hey, Noah, you can come out now."

And Noah said, "I can't, Lord. It isn't the first of the month yet."

And the Lord said, "Well, why don't we wait till next month around the twenty-seventh?" And so they did.

And everybody left and the animals went forth after their own kind again. Grace must have been relieved to have them find their own kind for a change. Seems like after all those days on the ark, they would have wanted something else to eat, though.

I wonder what Noah did with his dear little ark? Maybe he ran an ad in the paper and sold it kind of used. I guess someone must still be building them. My father said one time he got a car that was a real ark of a thing. I hope that doesn't mean we are going to have another flood. Seems like once is enough.

I won't worry till we quit having rainbows. That's what the Lord promised.

P.S. Lord, if you still have some extra kind lying around someplace, will you please drop it in our backyard? I'll take good care and water it. Then Mr. Hofhiser can offer it on a two-for-one sale. And could you please put more green in the rainbow? It's my favorite color.

Also, if you ever have another flood, will you please change the rules? That's because I have three goldfish. I sure would hate to leave one behind.

Chapter 15

Angels

There are many things about angels I do not understand. Like how come there are so many around at Christmas time and none at Easter? Also it must be very hard to carry their wings around all the time. That's why I don't want to be one.

When me and Lydia June played angels in the Christmas play one time, the coat hangers poked a hole in my back. Lydia June parked her bubble gum in one of hers so it wouldn't get lost. But when we walked out, the gum in her wing caught Johnny Belcher's wing. And when he went to raise his arms and "Hark!" the whole thing fell off—wings and all.

Does this happen in Heaven when you are floating from one cloud to another? Is this why some of them are called falling angels? I think I would rather settle for a seat next to Abraham, and let someone else do the flying.

Mrs. Cronk is always looking at Janie McIntyre and saying, "Isn't she a perfect angel?" If this is so, I'll never make it. I have tried spitting through my teeth and crossing my eyes like Janie does. But all I do is get all in a mess. I just hope the Lord Almighty doesn't have me down in his book to be a perfect angel. I would hate to tell him I can't do all those things.

My father says we aren't supposed to know all about angels until we get to Heaven. But then how will we know about when to "Hark!" and when to fly? I am sure the Lord Almighty must have a book that would help everyone who wants to be one.

I asked Mrs. Stillwater at the library if there was any book on how to be a perfect angel. Mrs. Stillwater looked at me and said if there was one, it sure wouldn't help me very much. Maybe because it's not written in American so I could understand it.

I asked Mrs Cronk what an archangel was, and she threw up her hands and said, "Heavens, child, it beats me." I got real upset. Aren't archangels supposed to be nice people? Mrs. Cronk must know something we don't know about.

I know an angel came in a dream to Joseph one time. Maybe Mrs. Cronk's archangel comes by and gives her a whack every once in a while. For what, I do not know. She's a nice Sunday school teacher most of the time. Except when we make those silly rolls for the heathen.

My father says Sunday school teachers have their place. I have looked all over the church and haven't found out where that is. Maybe us kids will have to help her find it.

P.S. Lord, I could help you write a book on how to be a perfect angel. I think you would want us to know before we got there. But could we please write it in American? I wouldn't want to write something I couldn't read. If you would like me to help you in this, will you please make it rain next Thursday?

P.P.S. Lord, could you maybe send me an angel in a dream just so I could meet one? Make it just an angel, though. I'm not so sure of the arch ones.

Chapter 16

Rummage Sales

Rummage sales are where everybody can bring all their things to. That's so they can go home with everybody else's. Until the next time. Like old Mr. Smith's lampshade with the red tassels. It has been there five times.

Mrs. Cronk says rummage sales "help the work of the Lord." That's why they bring old sweaters with holes in them and clothes that smell like our attic after a rain. The box in the church hall gets bigger and bigger until it can't stand it any longer. Neither can Mr. Berriman, our janitor. So they have a rummage sale.

Mr. Berriman says he thinks they are the work of the devil. He said people are like jello. They come in strawberry, lemon and cheap. I couldn't ask Mr. Hofhiser at the store about that. He might feel bad if he wasn't strawberry.

I don't know who rummage sales are supposed to help. Maybe the Lord Almighty feels sorry for the devil and gives him half.

I like the fish pond for us kids the best. We get to hold a pole over the curtain. Then maybe we will get dominoes with only a few

spots gone or a puzzle with a couple of pieces missing.

One day we had our own rummage sale. Lydia June brought her mother's teapot. Janie brought her aunt's big glass bowl. Johnny came with his father's hunting knife. And I took some of the Lord Almighty's grape juice from the dining room cupboard. And we all swapped.

The only one who was happy was the Lord Almighty. My father said our rummage sale wasn't the work of the Lord. I said, why. He got all red in the face and said he guessed because it wasn't held in the church. I said I thought the work of the Lord was everywhere like the Bible says.

The Sunday after the rummage sale, everybody comes to church looking like everybody else. Old Mr. Smith looks like Mr. Hofhiser in the blue shirt with the top button missing. And Burt Peasley's feet look like Mr. Smith's in the shoes with one heel gone. And they all stand and sing "Hallelujah! Amen."

P.S.   Lord, I know there must be rummage sales in Heaven. When my father asked old Mrs. Benson where she got all the things she brought in, she said, "Heaven only knows."

Chapter 17

The Devil

Whenever I try to ask about the devil, everyone says, "Sshhh!" Mrs. Cronk gets up and hurries to find a new thing for the heathen. Mr. Berriman leans so far in the rummage sale box, I can't talk to him. And my father says, how can he listen for word from the Lord if I'm asking about the devil? I say, while you're waiting around, can't you ask the Lord Almighty about him for me? And my father says, child, the Lord Almighty has nothing to DO with the devil.

I do not understand this. If rummage sales are the work of the devil like Mr. Berriman says, how come his box is in our church basement? The devil must be awful important to make everybody "Sshhh!" all the time. And he must be awful busy running a mosquito factory and a skunk factory so we can have lots of each.

My father says on Sunday sometimes, "Be careful when the devil taps you on the shoulder and winks his eye. Then he leads you up the path of sinning and you're a goner!" That makes all the sinners hurry up front while the "sent" and the "chosen" sing one more time.

I wish I knew what path it was the devil leads them up. I would sure stay away from it. But I sure know what to do if he taps me on the shoulder. I just won't turn around.

One day Lydia June and I practiced tapping, so we'd know what it felt like. Then we practiced leading each other up the path behind her house. But we couldn't practice the fiery pit 'cause there wasn't any. I wonder what everyone does when they get there? Maybe they have a big party and play Pin the Tail on the Donkey.

My father tells everybody the work of the devil goes on when you aren't even around. But if there isn't anybody there, how can you know about it?

I sure wish we could find someone to ask. If Burt Peasley knows of a back way into Heaven, maybe he knows about the path to sinning. I think I will ask him sometime.

If I can't find out before, maybe I can when I get to Heaven. I'll just unstop a window like the Lord Almighty did with Noah. Then I'll lean out and yell, "What goes on down there?" Then the devil and I will have a nice visit. After that, I'll know and the Lord Almighty will know and everybody will know.

P.S.   Lord, don't worry about it. When I get to Heaven, I'll find out for both of us.

Chapter 18

Going to Heaven

We played dying and going to Heaven last week. Johnny Belcher didn't want to be the one. But he can't sing "Just As I Am" like Lydia June. And he doesn't know the "gathered togethers" like me. So it was the only part left.

He said it might give him the creeps like passing the liver at Halloween. I told him it was the good part. Not everyone gets to die just when they feel like it. He said OK, if we didn't kiss him when he had his eyes shut. And if he could have some extra Kool-aid when he got through dying.

I got our biggest bed pillows and the blue blanket from the company bed. It looks like a going-to-Heaven blanket with its shiny blue edge. We put it behind the couch on the back porch.

Johnny said, "OK, stupid, what do I do now?"

Lydia June sighed and said, "Just act kind of droopy and tired. And then say, 'OK, Lord, I think I would like to be with you now.' And then I sing 'Just As I Am' while you just float up to the pearly gates."

Johnny said, "That's kind of silly. Can't I zoom up in a fiery rocket? Or take a 747?"

"Of course not," I said. "Burt Peasley is the only one who knows of another way. But no one will tell us what it is."

Johnny rolled his eyes and started the "OK, Lord." Lydia June sang while I put the lace curtain on. Then I started the "gathered togethers." That is really the part for my father's weddings. But it makes everybody happy to see the bride and groom leave for Niagara Falls. So I knew it would make everyone happy to see Johnny leave for Heaven.

I told Johnny to keep his eyes shut. Then I hurried so I could be St. Peter standing on the couch.

"You can get up now because you are in Heaven," I told him. "Swing back the pearly gates, Lydia June, so I can open the Big Book."

I opened the Sears catalog to the middle where all the lawn mowers are. "What is your name?" I asked.

Johnny giggled and rolled his eyes. "I'm Johnny Belcher and I want a big, big house and a big, big Honda to ride—and lots of chocolate ice cream sundaes every day—".

Just then my mother came out. She was kind of upset about her pillows and the going-to-Heaven blanket. I told her we were helping Johnny go to Heaven. She said some people needed all the help they could get. But not to use her good blanket to do it.

So we had to wait till another day so Johnny could finish dying.

We went out and lay in the grass to see if we could see Heaven. Lydia June was sure it was the big, big white cloud over Mr. Click's hardware store. It didn't look big enough to me. And Johnny said an awful thing. He said the cloud place looked sissy. Like it was only for girls. He said he'd rather go to the "other place." Then he could sit on the edge of the fiery pit and roast hot dogs.

I guess it really doesn't matter where Heaven is. I just know you will get Lydia June and me there. OK?

P.S.

Dear Lord Almighty,

There are still a few things I would like to know about, like—

1. Why can't we ever fall *up*?

2. Where do the flowers go when they aren't anymore?

3. Do animals get to be the "sent," too? Like the nice lion who didn't hurt Daniel in his den? And like my kitten, Harvey, who loves me?

4. Next time you make people out of clay—like Adam and Eve —could you use my favorite colors like orange and bright green?

5. Is your wife as nice as Noah's wife, Grace (you know, who took care of all the ark animals)? And does your wife get to listen to people sometimes like you do? I would like her to listen to me— especially at night.

I think that is all for now. Even though I don't understand everything, I want you to know I am still on your side.

Love,

Sarah Elizabeth